David Zippel

David Zippel's lyrics have won him a Tony® Award, two Academy Award® nominations, two GRAMMY Award® nominations, and three Golden Globe nominations. He is one of the few contemporary lyricists to have achieved success on Broadway, in film, and in pop music. Broadway: *City of Angels*, *The Goodbye Girl*, and *Barbara Cook: A Concert for the Theatre*. *The Woman in White* resulted in a #2 single on British pop charts and was nominated for five Olivier Awards, including Best Musical. Films: Disney's *Hercules*, Disney's *Mulan*, *The Swan Princess*, *Frankie and Johnny*, and *The Wedding Planner*. Off-Broadway: *Just So*, *It's Better with a Band*, *Diamonds*, and *A...My Name Is Alice*. His songs appear on more than 25 million CDs, including recordings by Stevie Wonder, Christina Aguilera, Mel Tormé, Ricky Martin, 98 Degrees, Cleo Laine, Linda Eder, Nancy LaMott, Sarah Brightman, and Barbara Cook. He is the lyricist and director of *Princesses*, a musical adaptation of *A Little Princess*, which is bound for Broadway. The Lincoln Center American Songbook is presenting an evening of David's songs on February 24, 2007. A graduate of Harvard Law School, he is delighted not to practice law.

Larry Gelbart

Larry Gelbart wrote the book for the musical *City of Angels* and, with Burt Shevelove, *A Funny Thing Happened on the Way to the Forum*. Other stage credits include *The Conquering Hero*, *Mastergate*, *Jump!*, *Power Failure*, and *Like Jazz*. Among his screenplays are *Tootsie*; *Oh, God!*; *Movie, Movie*; and *The Wrong Box*. In television he wrote for "Caesar's Hour" before creating "M*A*S*H" and "United States," as well as the teleplays "Barbarians at the Gate," "Weapons of Mass Distraction," and "And Starring Pancho Villa as Himself."

CITY OF ANGELS

CONTENTS

CITY OF ANGEL'S THEME

Music by CY COLEMAN
Lyrics by DAVID ZIPPEL

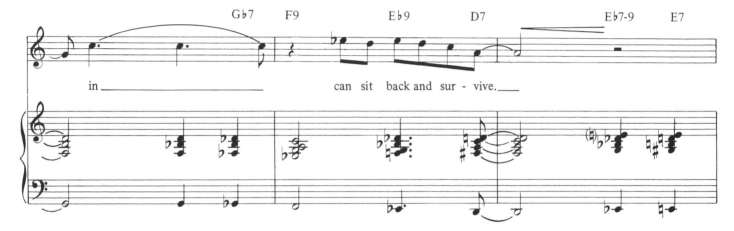

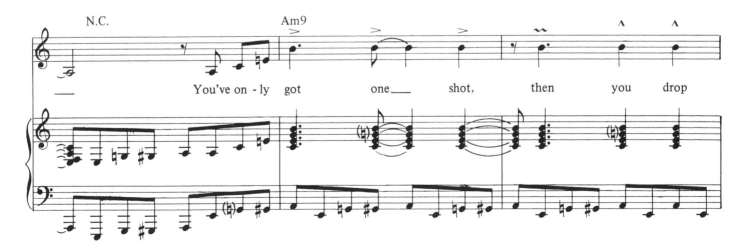

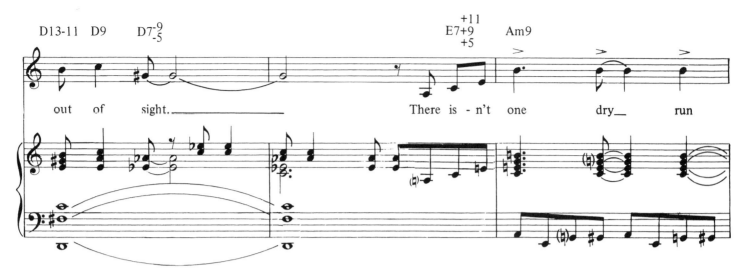

out of sight._____ There is - n't one dry__ run

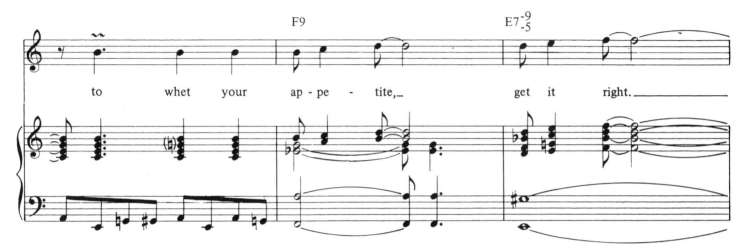

to whet your ap - pe - tite,__ get it right._____

We're on the edge of a cliff___ set up to take the ul-ti-mate fall.___

So have a last cig-ar-ette and bet it all._____

Just go out and keep swing-in'_____ till you hear the bell toll.___

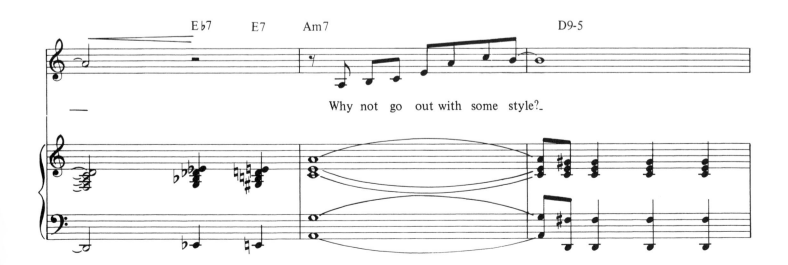

Why not go out with some style?_

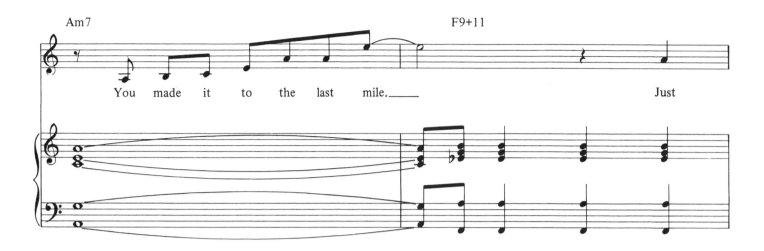

You made it to the last mile._____ Just

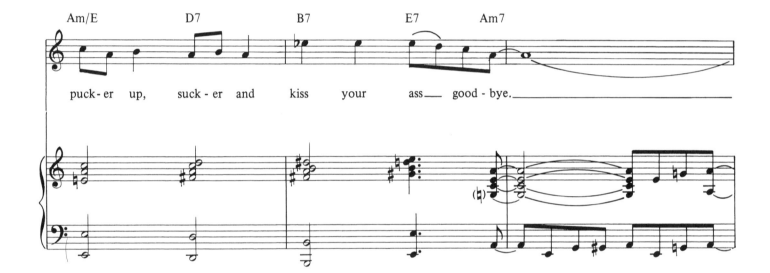

puck-er up, suck-er and kiss your ass___ good-bye._____

WHAT YOU DON'T KNOW ABOUT WOMEN

Music by CY COLEMAN
Lyrics by DAVID ZIPPEL

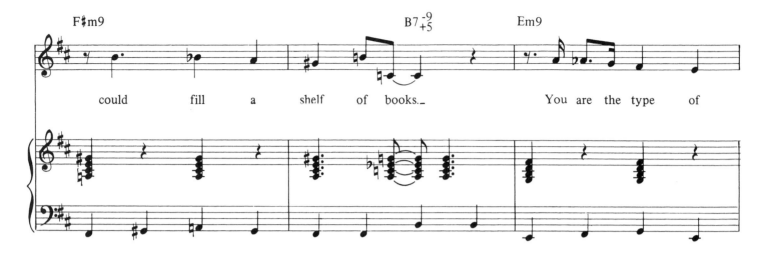

could fill a shelf of books._ You are the type of

man who looks_ for un - der - stand - ing lo - vers____

But ne - ver un - der - stands the girl_ who lies be - neath the cov -

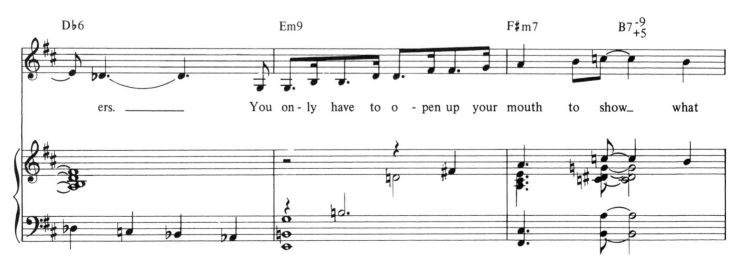

ers. ____ You on - ly have to o - pen up your mouth to show_ what

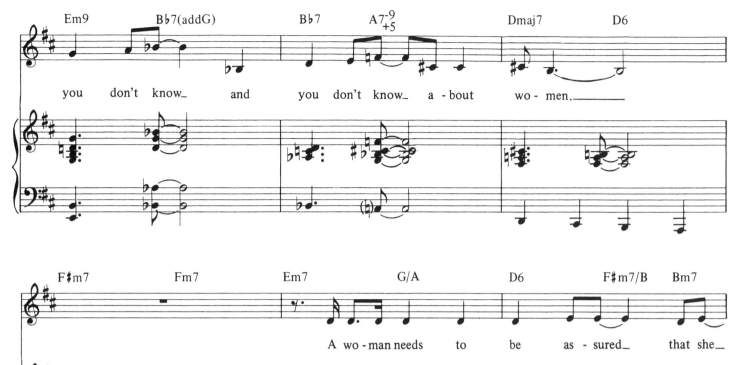

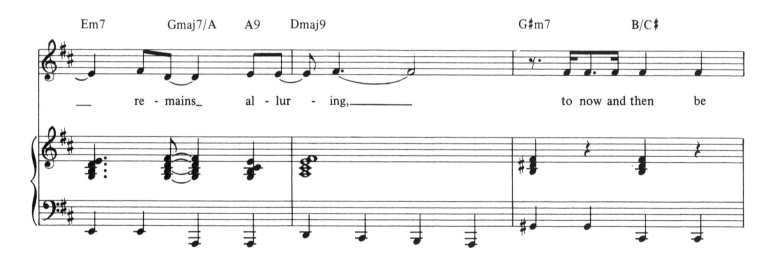

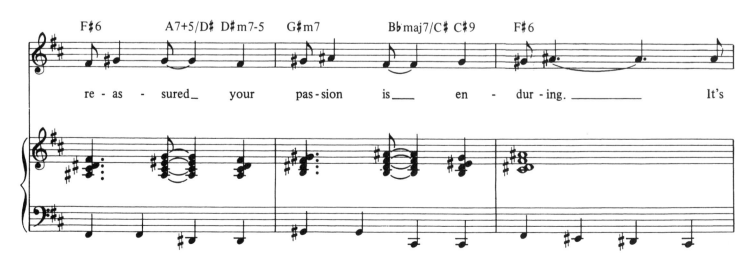

we'll come run - ning to___ you._____ Throw in some truth for

at - mos - phere___ but we can see right through__ you._____ And

ev' - ry hol - low com - pli - ment and phrase de - fines___ and

un - der - lines___ what you don't know___ a - bout wo - men._____

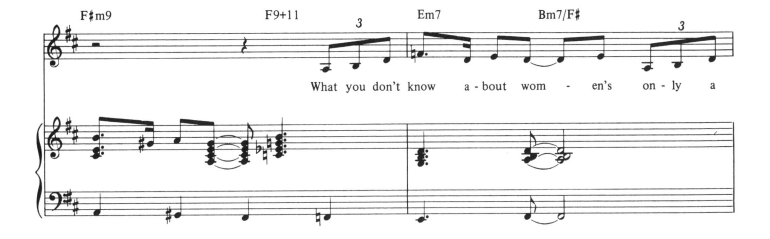

F#m9　　　F9+11　　　Em7　　　Bm7/F#

What you don't know a - bout wom - en's on - ly a

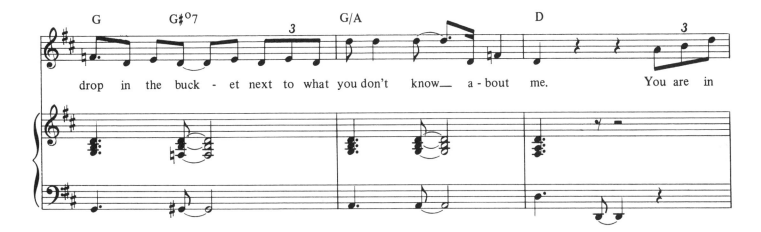

G　　G#°7　　G/A　　D

drop in the buck - et next to what you don't know____ a - bout me. You are in

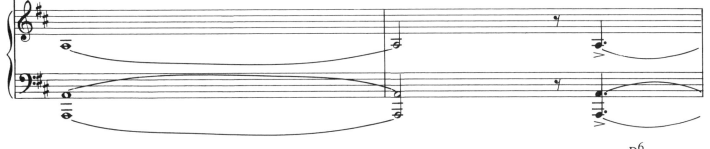

Bm7/E　　No chord

need of a lit - tle en -light' -ning on la -dies and love but you can't see, what you don't

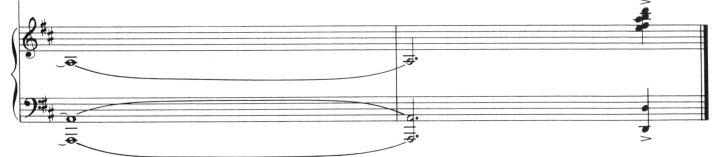

D⁶/₉

know a -bout wom-en is fright-'ning and you don't know noth -in' a -bout me.

WITH EVERY BREATH I TAKE

Music by CY COLEMAN
Lyrics by DAVID ZIPPEL

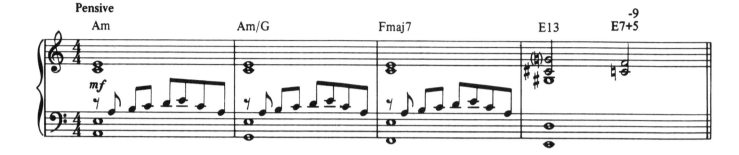

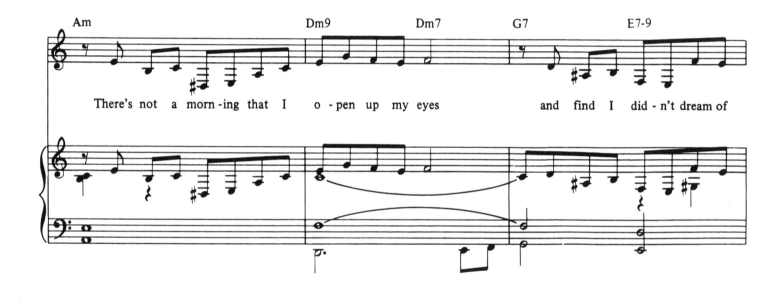

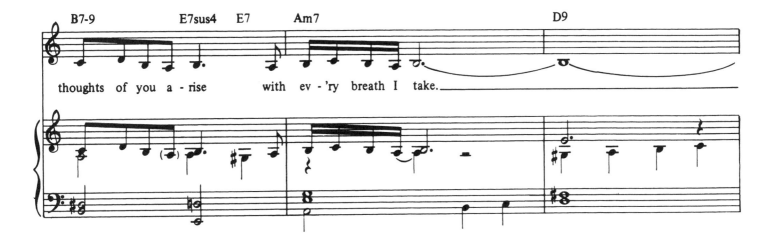

thoughts of you a - rise with ev -'ry breath I take.___

At an - y time or

place I close my eyes and see your face and

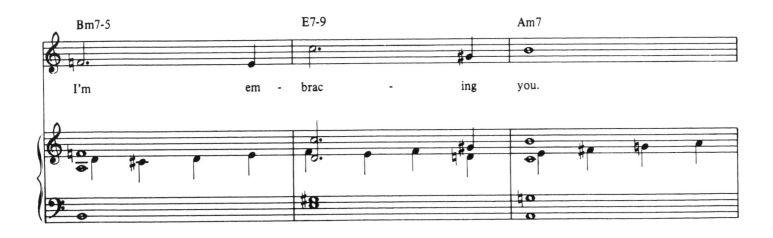

I'm em - brac - ing you.

If on-ly I be-lieved that dreams come

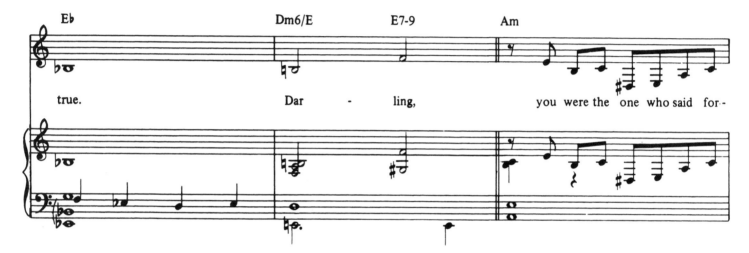

true. Dar - ling, you were the one who said for-

ev - er from the start and I've been drift - ing since you've

gone, out on a lone-ly sea that on-ly you can chart.

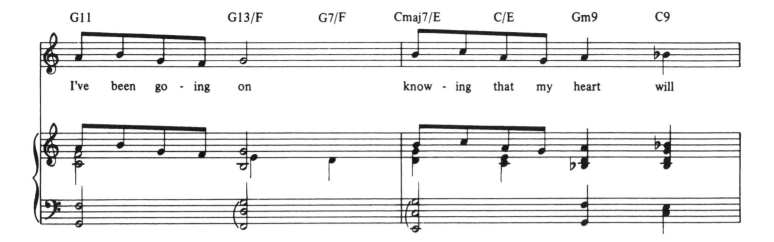

I've been go - ing on

know - ing that my heart will

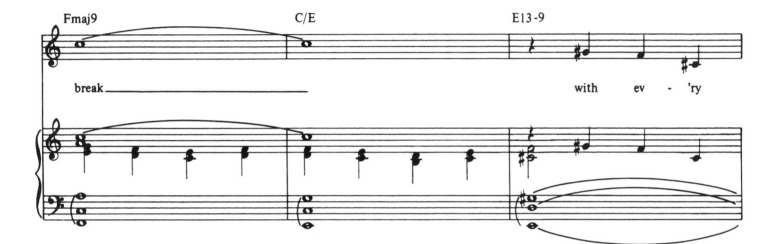

break

with ev - 'ry

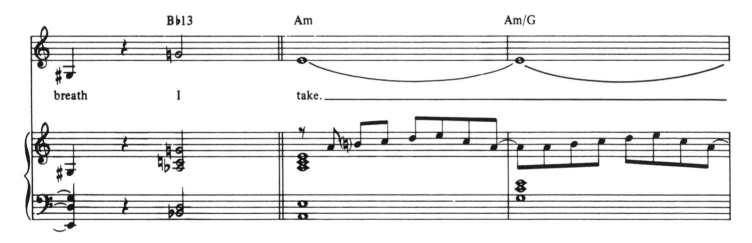

breath I take.

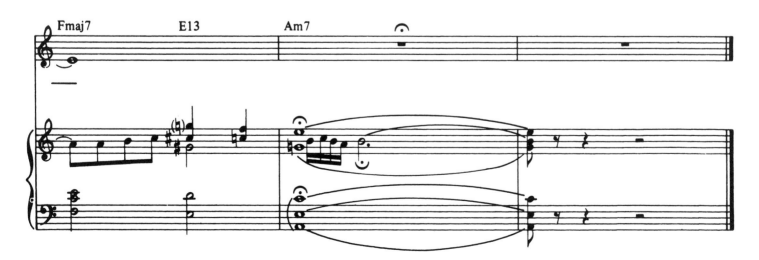

EVERYBODY'S GOTTA BE SOMEWHERE

Music by CY COLEMAN
Lyrics by DAVID ZIPPEL

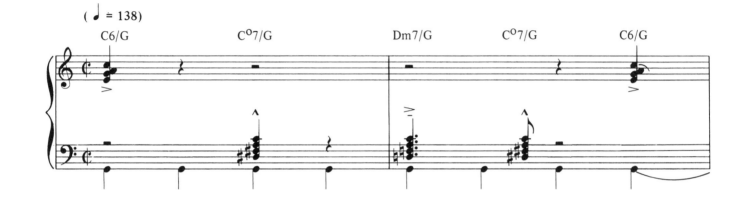

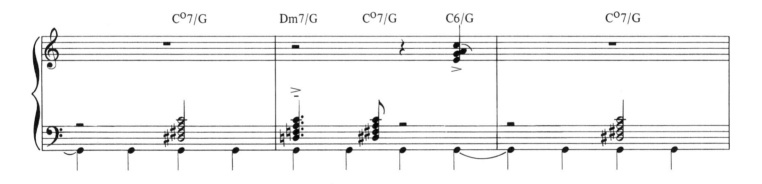

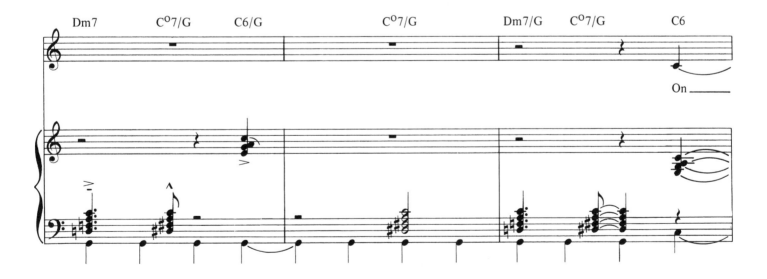

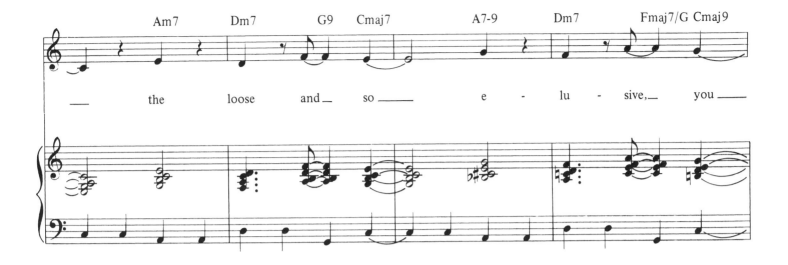

the loose and— so ——— e - lu - sive,— you ———

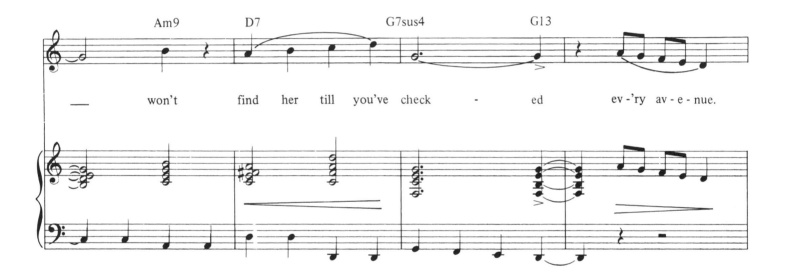

—— won't find her till you've check - ed ev -'ry av - e - nue.

Like a dia - mond— in ——— a coal mine,— she's ——

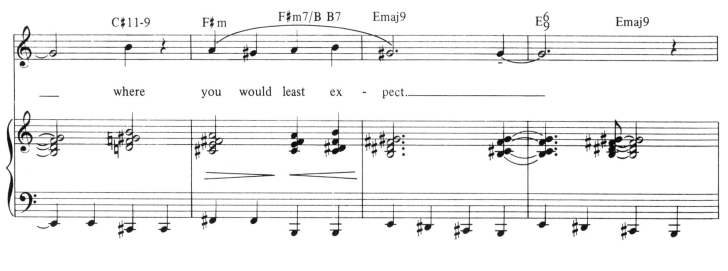

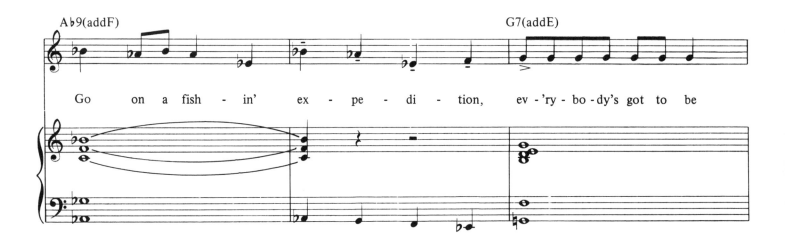

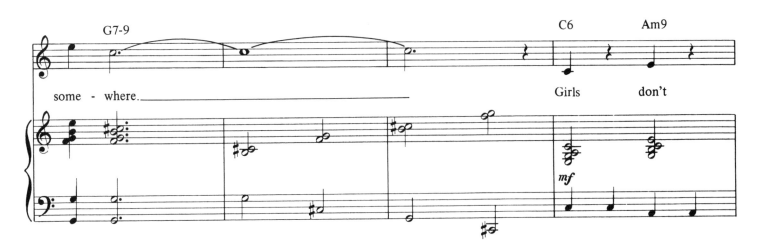

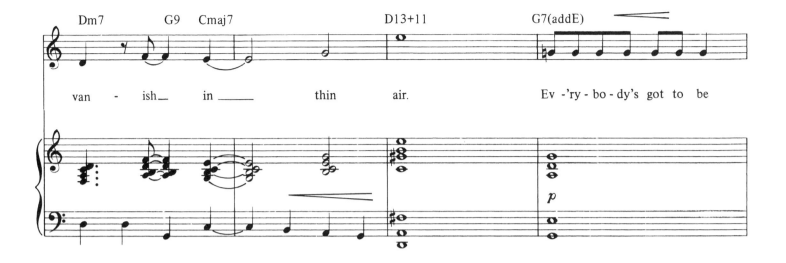

van - ish___ in ___ thin air. Ev -'ry - bo - dy's got to be

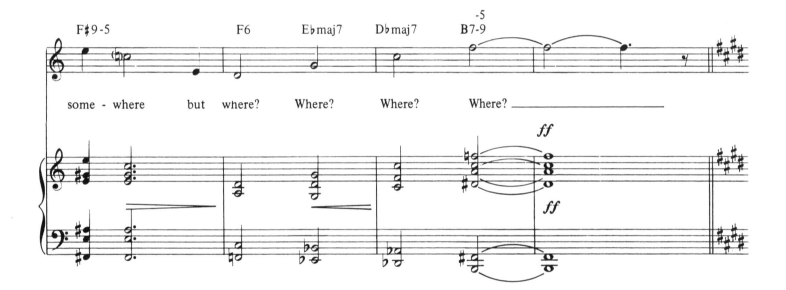

some - where but where? Where? Where? Where? _____

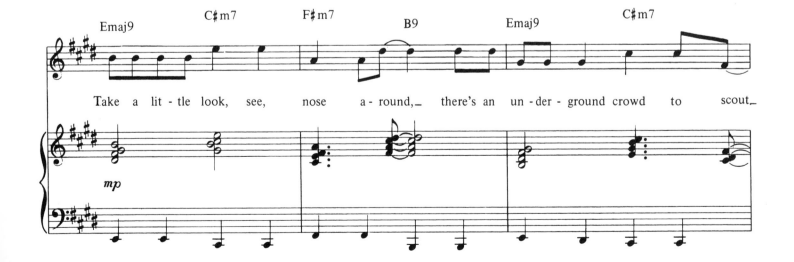

Take a lit - tle look, see, nose a - round,___ there's an un - der - ground crowd to scout

Use a lit-tle in-tu-i-tion if you wish___ your

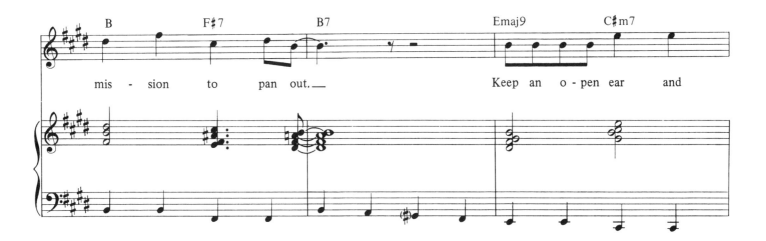

mis - sion to pan out.___ Keep an o-pen ear and

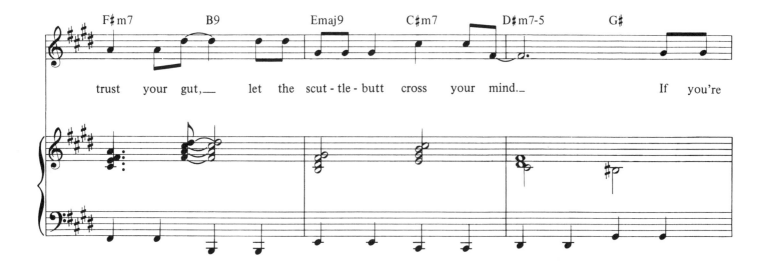

trust your gut,___ let the scut - tle - butt cross your mind.___ If you're

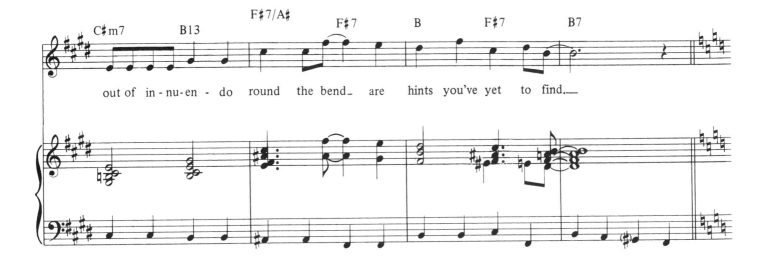

out of in-nu-en-do round the bend_ are hints you've yet to find,_

Stay right on her trail. This to-ma-to is a hot po-ta-to.

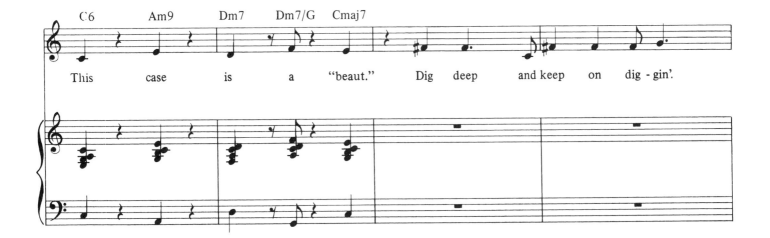

This case is a "beaut." Dig deep and keep on dig-gin'.

28

She's the ho - ly grail, she's a nee - dle in hay - stack heav - en.

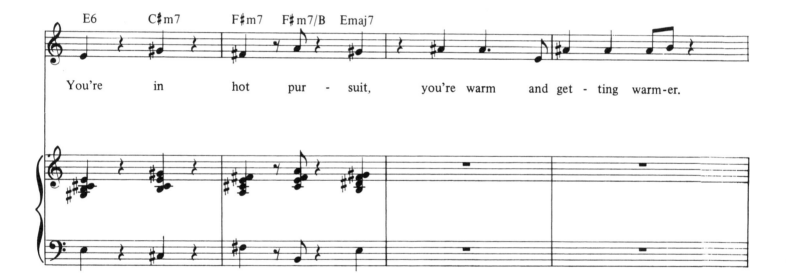

You're in hot pur - suit, you're warm and get - ting warm-er.

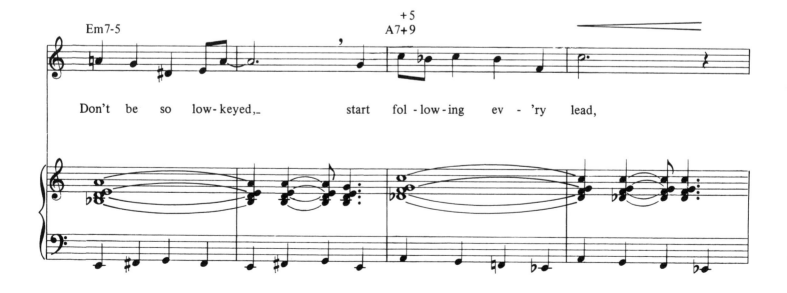

Don't be so low-keyed,_ start fol - low-ing ev - 'ry lead,

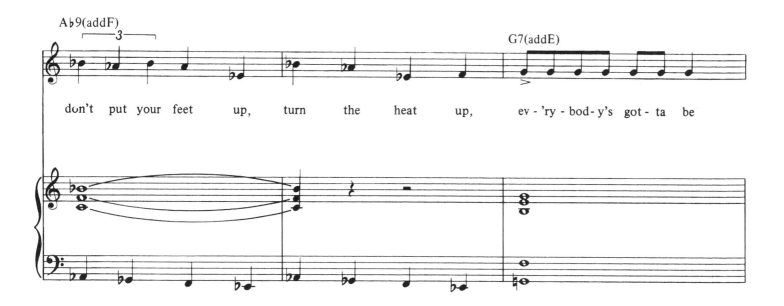

don't put your feet up, turn the heat up, ev-'ry-bod-y's got-ta be

some - where._____ Girls don't

van - ish___ in ___ thin air._____ First you got-ta look

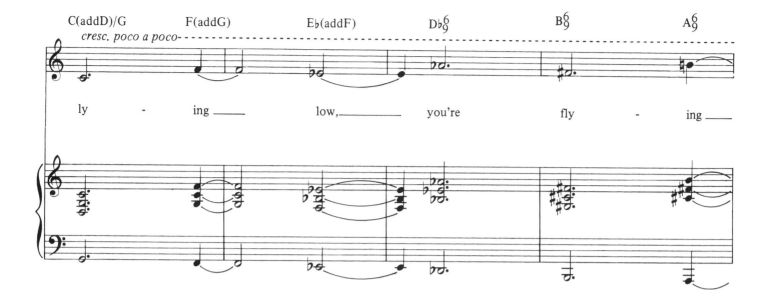

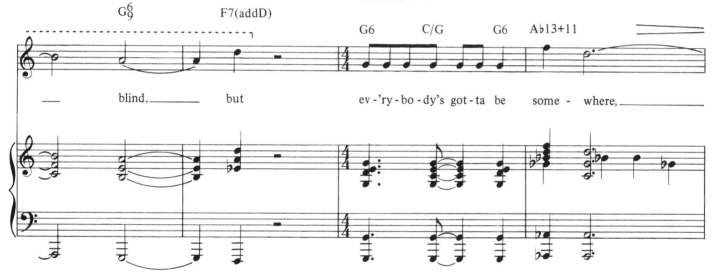

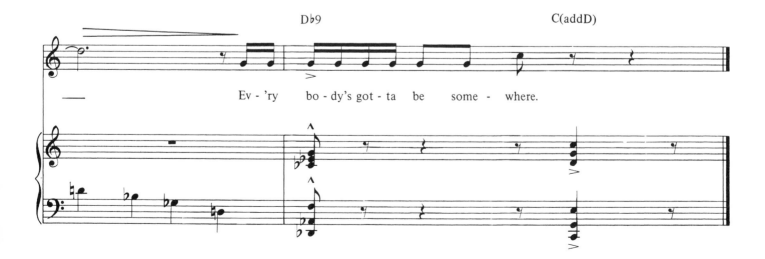

LOST AND FOUND

Music by CY COLEMAN
Lyrics by DAVID ZIPPEL

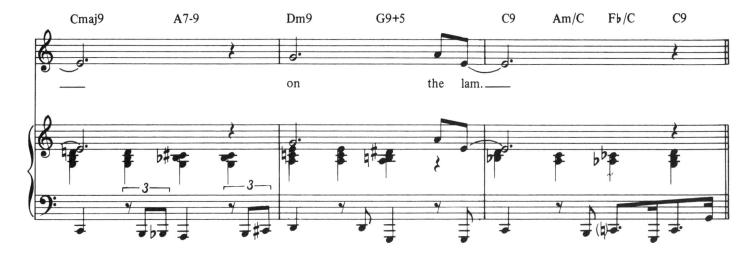

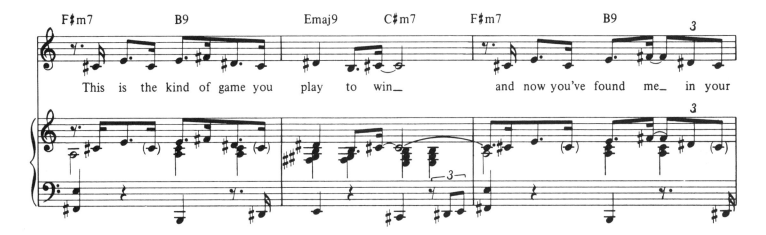

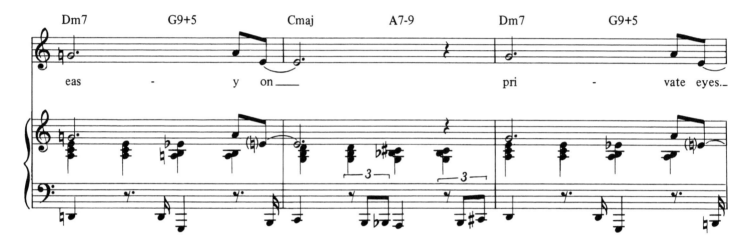

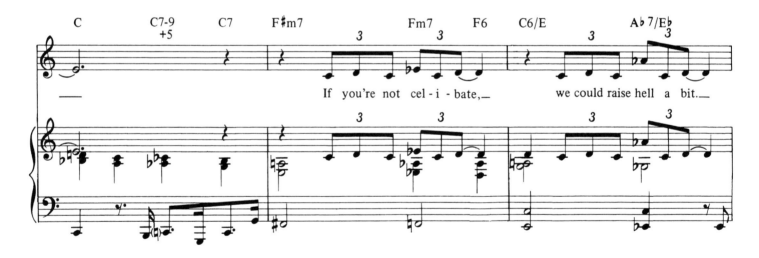

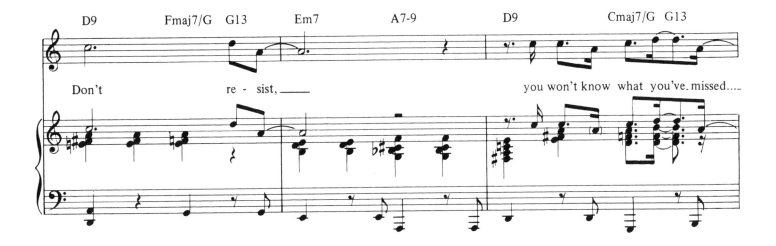

Don't re - sist, _____ you won't know what you've missed....

You'll_nev-er tame me but__ you can claim me at the

lost and found. _____

8va -

YOU'RE NOTHING WITHOUT ME

Music by CY COLEMAN
Lyrics by DAVID ZIPPEL

Moderately bright

You are some gum - shoe, you just don't think_ well.
You are so jeal - ous of just my track rec - ord.

Get this dumb gum - shoe, you come_ from my ink - well.
Tol - stoy, do tell_ us, your fee - ble hack rec - ord.

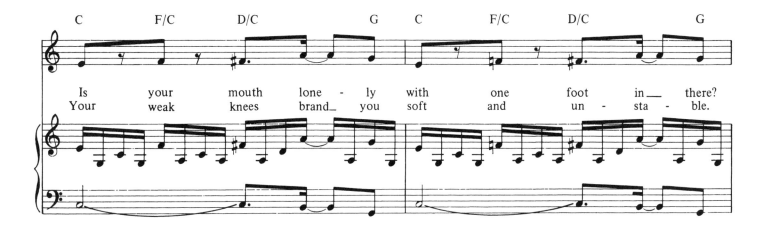

C   F/C   D/C   G   C   F/C   D/C   G

Is your mouth lone - ly with one foot in __ there?
Your weak knees brand __ you soft and un - sta - ble.

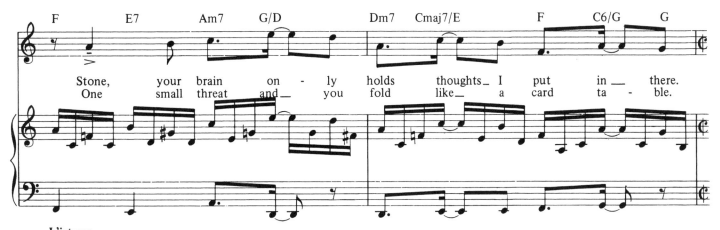

F   E7   Am7   G/D   Dm7   Cmaj7/E   F   C6/G   G

Stone, your brain on - ly holds thoughts __ I put in __ there.
One small threat and __ you fold like __ a card ta - ble.

L'istesso
$(\circ = \circ)$

E7   Am

Just what you are I'll spell out. __
You drool at my ad - ven - tures, __

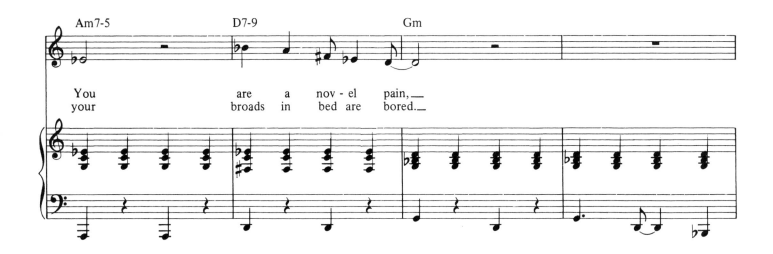

Am7-5   D7-9   Gm

You are a nov - el pain, __
your broads in bed are bored. __

tell you you're out of my mind. A show off, a

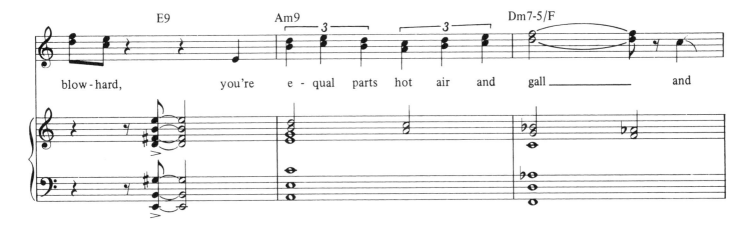

blow - hard, you're e - qual parts hot air and gall _____ and

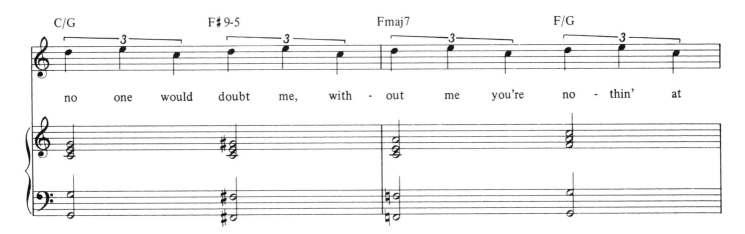

no one would doubt me, with - out me you're no - thin' at

A tempo

all. _____

You're in my plot___ I'm still your cre - a - tor.
*You are some part - ner, you think we're e - qual.
**All my day - dreams___ be - gin and end on___ you;

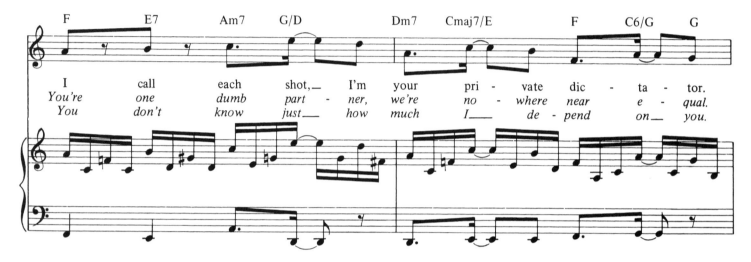

I call each shot,___ I'm your pri - vate dic - ta - tor.
You're one dumb part - ner, we're no - where near e - qual.
You don't know just___ how much I___ de - pend on___ you.

You are so thick,___ you eat, breathe, sleep fic - tion.
You are so jeal - ous of my track rec - ord;
I am sky high___ when I spend time with___ you;

I'm your meal tick - et, knee deep___ in cheap fic - tion.
why don't you tell___ us your fee - ble hack rec - ord.
I'm in or - bit___ the in - stant___ that I'm with___ you.

*Alternate lyrics for "YOU'RE NOTHING WITHOUT ME" (If alternate lyrics are used, begin song at this point.)
**Alternate lyrics for "I'M NOTHING WITHOUT YOU"

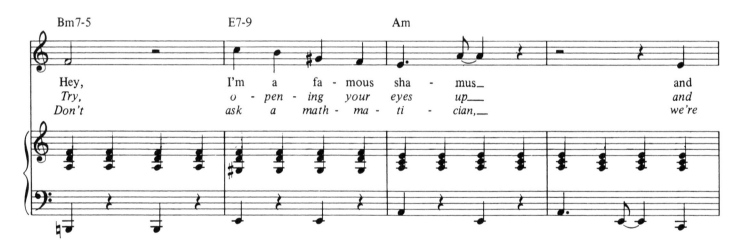

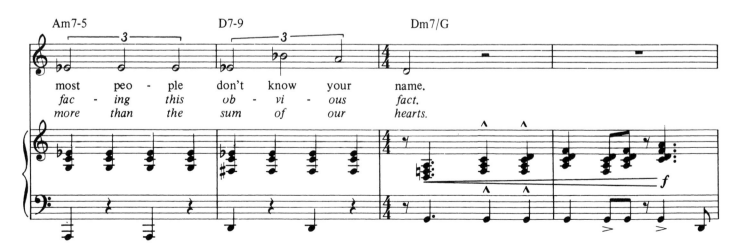

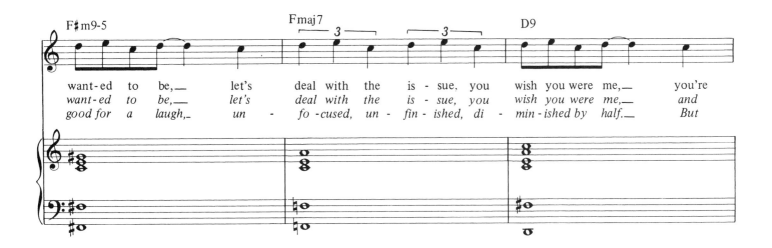

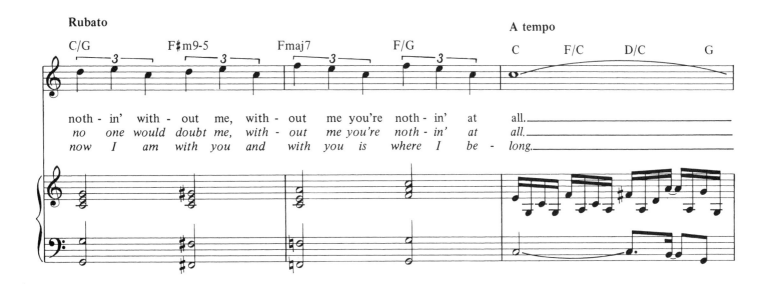

STAY WITH ME

Music by CY COLEMAN
Lyrics by DAVID ZIPPEL

I'm in a

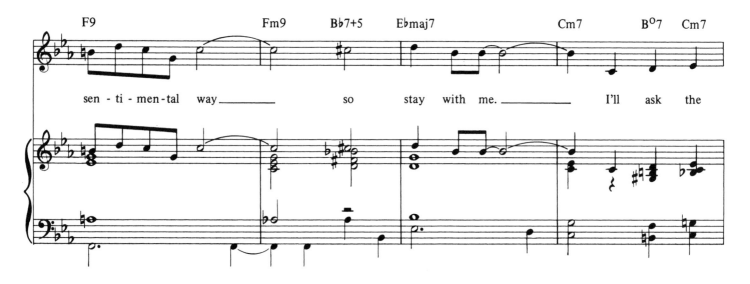

sen - ti - men - tal way_____ so stay with me._____ I'll ask the

or - ches - tra to play _____ your fav - 'rite song. _____

Thoughts that we would blush to say come eas-i-ly in song, ___

___ so why the rush ___ to say so long? ___

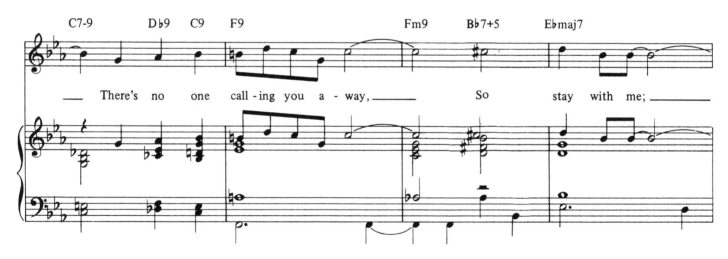

___ There's no one call-ing you a-way, ___ So stay with me; ___

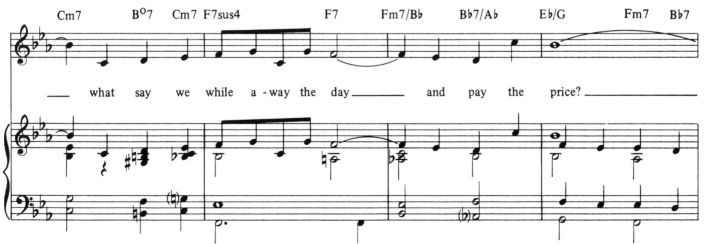

___ what say we while a-way the day ___ and pay the price? ___

YOU CAN ALWAYS COUNT ON ME

Music by CY COLEMAN
Lyrics by DAVID ZIPPEL

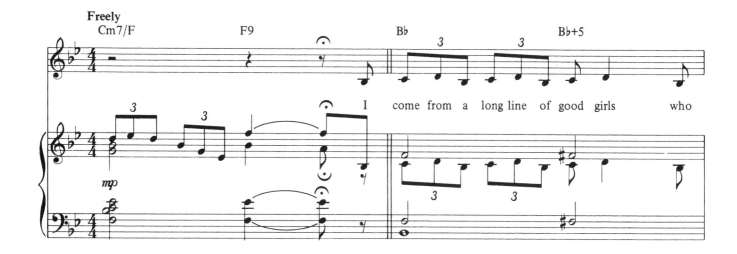

right, but what good does it do me a - lone on a Sat - ur - day night?

Moderately

I don't need a map, I nat -'ral - ly head for the dead end street.___
mat - ter of fact, if you want an ill - fat - ed love af - fair, ___
my kind of dame no doubt will die out like the di - no - saurs, ___

You can al - ways count on me.___ I'm
you can al - ways count on me.___ Though
you can al - ways count on me.___ I'm

al - ways on top for ro - mance or choc -'late that's bit - ter - sweet.___
else I at - tract the guys who are long - ing to do my hair.___
I've made a name with ho - tel de - tect - ives who break down doors.___

To Coda ⊕

You can al - ways count on me. ___
You can al - ways count on me.___

A ___

I

go for the riff - raff who's treat - ing me so ___ so; when I can play the se - cond fid - dle

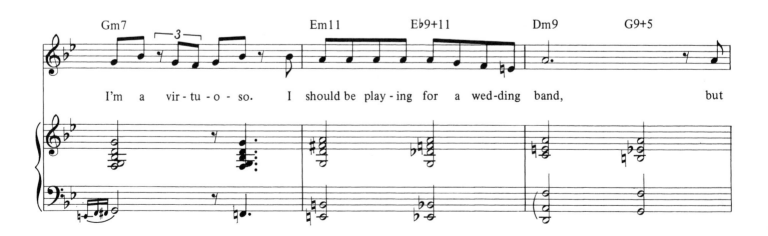

I'm a vir - tu - o - so. I should be play - ing for a wed - ding band, but

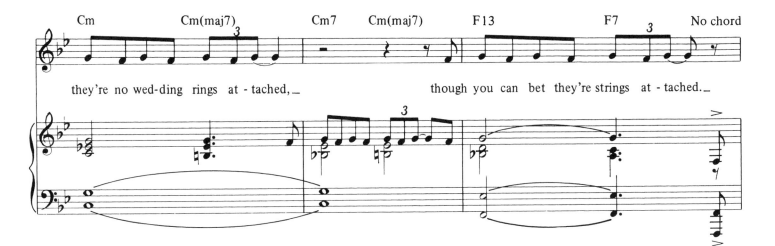

they're no wed-ding rings at-tached,_ though you can bet they're strings at-tached._

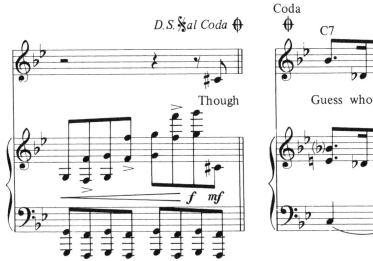

D.S. %al Coda ⊕ Coda ⊕

Though

Guess who they ex-pect to see?_

You can al-ways count on, bet a large a-mount on, you can al-ways count on me!_

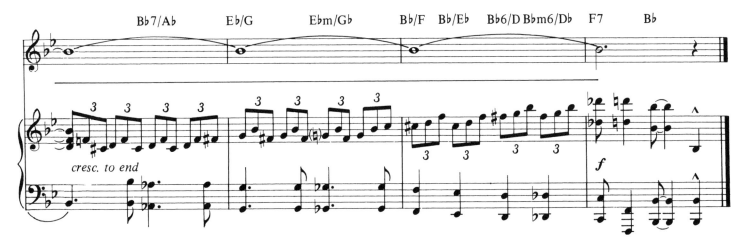

cresc. to end

ALAURA'S THEME

Music by CY COLEMAN
Lyrics by DAVID ZIPPEL

long _____ to be be - side her? Night af - ter night, _____ she

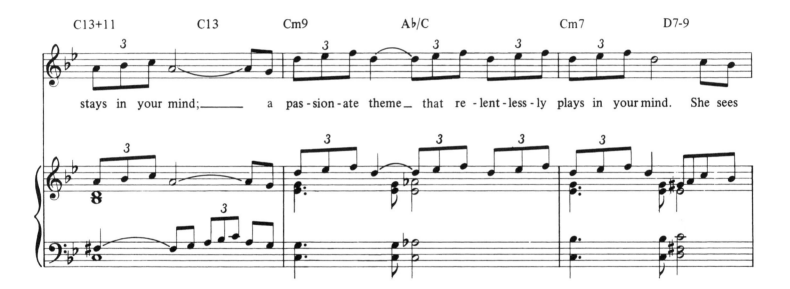

stays in your mind; _____ a pas - sion - ate theme _ that re - lent - less - ly plays in your mind. She sees

in - to your soul; _____ she knows you so well, _____ no won - der at all ____ that you're un - der a

54

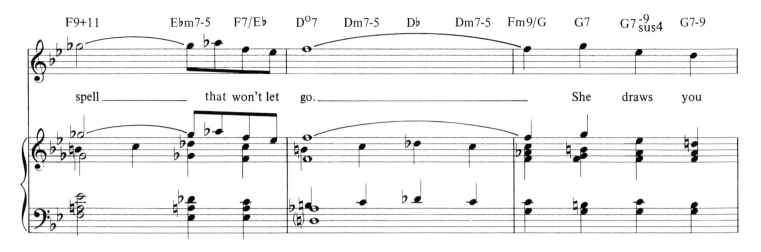

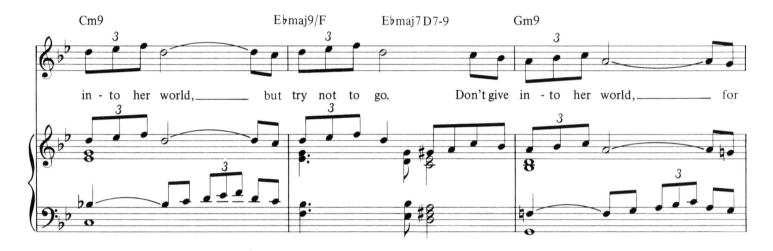

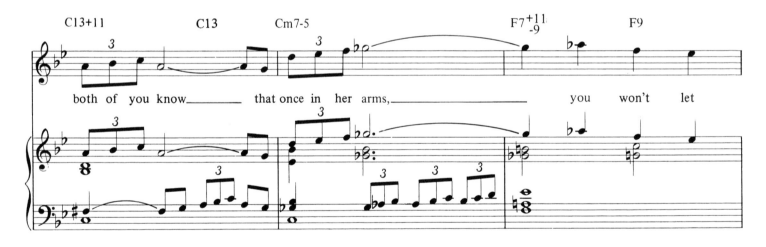

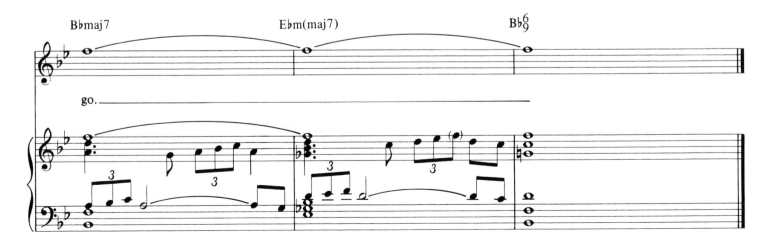

L.A. BLUES

Music by CY COLEMAN
Lyrics by DAVID ZIPPEL

Medium Blues

die. _____ I've got those L. A. blues. _____ I can't dis-

pell those L. A. blues. _____ Why'd I an - swer that call _____ from the

coast _____ just to lie _____ by a pool _____ till I roast? _____ This af-

fair _____ had be - gun _____ as my day _____ in the sun; _____ I was

toast __ of the town, __ now I'm toast. _____ I've got those L. A. blues. __

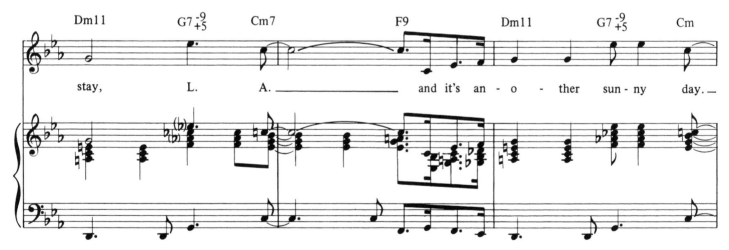

_____ Those gone to hell in L. A. blues. _____ I'm here to

stay, L. A. _____ and it's an - o - ther sun - ny day. __

FUNNY

Music by CY COLEMAN
Lyrics by DAVID ZIPPEL

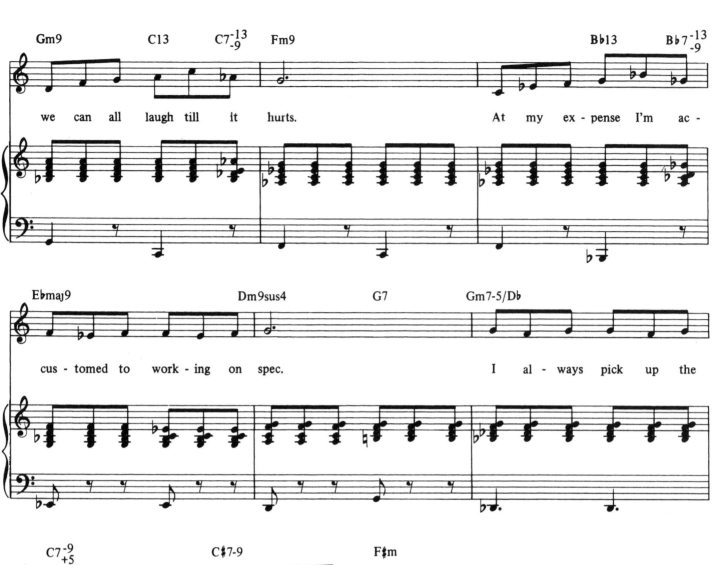

we can all laugh till it hurts. At my ex - pense I'm ac -

cus - tomed to work - ing on spec. I al - ways pick up the

check. I think it's fun - ny.

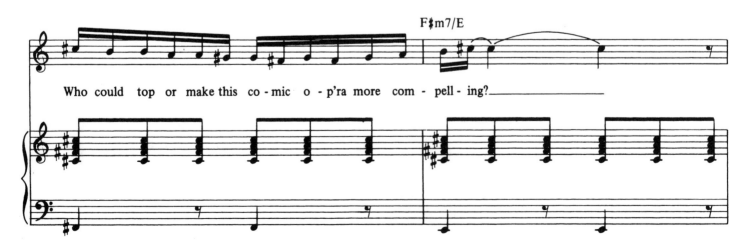

Who could top or make this co - mic o - p'ra more com - pell - ing?

You could weave in some de - ceit to e - ven up the score._____

You'd have us all on the floor, that would be roar - ing - ly

fun - ny._____ Sad e - nough, my life's a joke that suf - fers in the tell - ing,_____

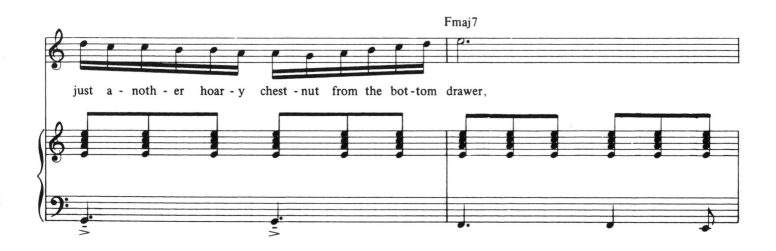

just a - noth - er hoar - y chest - nut from the bot - tom drawer,

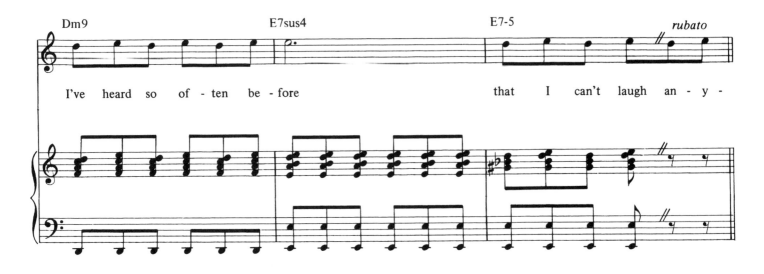

I've heard so of - ten be - fore

that I can't laugh an - y -

a tempo

more.

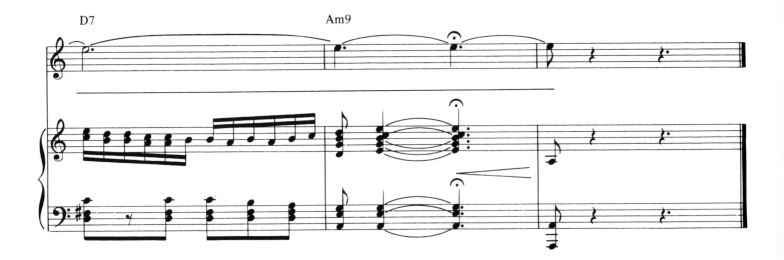